The Truth Of Seasons

poems by

Laverne Frith

Finishing Line Press
Georgetown, Kentucky

The Truth Of Seasons

ACKNOWLEDGMENTS

"The Vernal Pools": *Avocet, A Journal of Nature Poems*
"In Muted Light" & "Terzanelle For The Advent Of Winter": *CFCP, Inc.,
Prizewinning Poems*
"Icicles In The Pyracantha" & "In My Saucer": *Song of the San Joaquin*
"Drawing Water": *Louisiana Literature*

Editor: Christen Kincaid

Cover Art: Laverne Frith

Author Photo: Carol Frith

Cover Design: Elizabeth Maines

Printed in the USA on acid-free paper.
Order online: www.finishinglinepress.com
          also available on amazon.com

Author inquiries and mail orders:
Finishing Line Press
P. O. Box 1626
Georgetown, Kentucky 40324
U. S. A.

Table of Contents

Within the transitory nature of living,
to all we hold so dear

Down The Street From Us, Hanging Over The Church, The Full Moon Of Mid-January

positioned as though staking a claim
on space, filled as it is with all

its insinuations of light, and those
illusions that do not attach must

indeed be a resulting bounce of light
that creates the illusion, at least,

of penumbra, something of a partial
surround, though transitory, still

an attachment that adds to the naturalness
of it all, that assures in the heart

a promise of some permanence,
of the possibilities of future repetitions,

a lightness that, in a strange way,
amplifies all the surrounding darkness.

All of this, just down the street—
an imaginary tether, connecting

earth to sky.

Name It Longing

Some accepted the challenge.
I moved on, not understanding,

not accepting, how the town grew,
how it stayed the same.

In the years that followed,
more migrations, less remaining.

On some days now I just reflect,
as though somehow, after

all this time, something clarifies:
most of what pushed me, all

the old examples simply burning through—
those missing, those forever gone.

Only In March

and only then will you see
such a morning, the sun falling

in such a manner on the light green leaves
of the ivy clinging to the brick wall,

that you can see those highlights also
in the white blossoms of the nearby yarrow,

as the early spring breeze grabs
the cornucopia of growth all around

and induces its gentle swaying.
And don't you wonder about

the larger picture—how forces
far away, beneath the surface,

above the surface, are exerting influences,
how the beginnings of melt and surges

of the spirit begin to tell the inclusive story—
how the new sounds beg and beg

for translation.

The Whipping Rains Of March

"Where are the songs of spring? Ay, where are they?"
(Keats)

We count the days of mounting rain,
relentless in their wrath, the pounding

drumbeat all too familiar now, the soggy
lawns and puddled water a testament—

the swollen rivers brim with false comforts,
the algal grasses almost eerie in the misty light.

We learn slowly how monsoonal flows complicate
in their passage. The bravest of the birds

now search and search in confusion, thankful
for the turning, unsure just how much of it

belongs to the songs of spring.

The Vernal Pools

The white and the discordant clouds
reflect in the vernal pools, range and range

of light—how they dissipate and fracture
in the water's depth, in their contained

syllables. They speak of events to come.
And near the vernal pools is a stand

of trees separate from the land, the clouds,
the sky. And there is that sheen the sun

has so generously provided between the rains.
The rest is a waiting game, portents

of more to come: that gathering of the
cumulus, a clump of cloud here, a clump

there. Each vernal pool hunkers in its
humble space, containing each ominous sign

of the day's remembrance, the transiency
of its forgetting.

Spring Trees

The white trees, the white blooming trees—
so many in a cluster. Each ball-like bloom

an island unto itself, although they flourish
in community as well. Even the small

children stand in awe of this new brightness.
And the tulip tree in the neighbor's lawn,

with a blanket of its white and purple blooms
already on the grasses . . . . The mild winter

has left us with this plethora of blooming,
that fills us with all those urgencies,

now emanating from the auras
of this viridescent and resonant spring.

Drawing Water

"This is how we do it," Aunt Emma would say,
loosening the rope and bucket from their

holder, dropping the tethered bucket into
the depth of the well. We would hear the splash,

sense the tug as the bucket sank and filled.
Then the difficult pull, bringing

bucket and water to the top, to steady it
so as not to waste its cargo. It took two hands

for her to carry it back to the steps of her
one-room school house. The children lined

up in single file, each receiving the dipper
in turn. This is how she refreshed the classes

in the heat of late May. This is how I learned about
Aunt Emma, learned so much more about water.

By Command

I followed my father on those journeys
through the woods, over the obstacles,

through the weeds and the grasses,
the hidden depressions and mounds,

through the crunch and crunch of leaves,
through the repeated sounds of gunshot

as he felled animal after animal,
and, each time, I felt the added weight

of them in the pouched canvas jacket:
the birds, the squirrels, the rabbits,

all commingled as if in a natural order,
all joined in a community of blood.

Whenever I hesitated, he would order
me onward. I knew from long practice

that the discipline would likely strengthen
me, but I could not suspect just how much

it made me know for sure the real difference
between life and death.

Once More The Wilds

the pathless woods, the tangles
in the briers, the sweetness there
literally hanging for the taking:

luscious blackberries
so thick we filled our baskets
in minutes, then contemplated

the long and difficult way out,
filled with itchiness, mosquitoes,
and endless gnats.

We remembered that sunny
afternoon—how we longed
so much for something

we knew, that would not wait.

Report On An Eventless Summer Afternoon

A rabbit crossing a field on a hot summer afternoon
is hardly an event.

A rabbit crossing a railroad track after crossing
a field on a hot summer afternoon is hardly an event.

And the fact that the heat would pay no attention
to the actions of that rabbit on that hot afternoon
is hardly an event.

But here, in the restless West, it is so easy
to go astray on a summer afternoon—ergo the report.

Storage Shed Relics

Who saved them I am not sure: mother,
my sisters, nephew? So many of Dad's
things in that box, things he collected

over the years; such an array:
knives, watches, pipes, tobacco,
tools, key chains, boxes of matches,

eyeglasses, spats, shoe polish,
medicines, photographs without names,
ticket stubs from train trips,

a few bullets, VFW buttons, field
glasses, a rabbit's foot on a chain,
letters already yellowed and faint.

I examine them one by one, as if
each can contribute something unique
to the language, would have something

special to say to me now that their
time is past. I need the affirmations
I am sure they hold—things that will

connect, and possibly reconnect
that lost world.

Summer Trauma At A Small Farm Outside Of Muskogee

In the middle of a sweltering August,
when there were no thoughts or hope

for water from the skies, no thought
at all, I remember when someone looked

across a long field and saw something
strange, yet familiar, forming in the distance,

truly forming as though a hidden hand
were shaping it, letting it move with a mind

of its own, to shift, sort of, to enlarge
and darken, and kind of lean in our direction,

the light of the afternoon suddenly
waning, diminishing our view of the sun,

as our afternoon filled with the knowledge
of storm, that special storm that would send

all of us scurrying to the cellar, sounding
the alarums, and taking with us

whatever we could.

In Muted Light
after pastel landscape by Terry Pappas

Along the river path are stands of trees,
impressionistic wisps of grass around
them, and a thick carpet of tangles

extending down the bank from the meander
of the path. The missing walkers have
traversed this just to see, at this bend,

and elsewhere, how the river rushes
and cavorts, and at times, settles.
And across the river in the distance,

other trees stand in mock repetition
and perhaps, there, too, secret trails
where walkers stare across. For this

is a river to fish from either side,
so few of them this close to a city.
This is a river to wish and dream by,

and a river to remember the times of
casting a line. Yet the river flows
mute today. And this trail, this

afternoon, finds itself in partial
shadow, but with spots of irregular
light Monet would have loved.

Of Homecoming

Each one of us is bound to forget something,
something about being there—oh so young,

all too eager, too ready to take on the world.
Remember then the parents in their prime,

and how and when we budded, in time, in time,
remember how eagerly we sprang from the nest,

though a bit uncertain, with the first blush
of the world in our face. But now that we have

weathered, have faced certain tests, we turn
once again to memory, to that bastion of love

called home. Try, if you will, to remember
when the old persimmon tree did its very best

to announce the fall.

In My Saucer

I am comforted by this curled brown leaf,
stiff yet fragile as any other of the magnolia's

offerings, resting so easily in its deep dark
brilliant-brown ebullience, with only the lighter

colored stem and veins to assuage the mood, lend
a lighter tone to its escape, one among thousands

blown unceremoniously to earth. I continue to eat
my breakfast, letting the whole picture of that

magnolia tree unfold again, letting me feel the
impulse to reach down and grab this near perfect

leaf and bring it home, selected over all the others
as if deified, made precious, when in truth,

in a few days, it, too, will escape the memory
along with the others; and even as this breakfast

draws to a close, that magnolia surrenders
even more—its prelude to new beginnings.

Crossing Over

In the misremembered light of early fall,
even the birch leaves hesitate. They gradually

begin to dip their tips. Suddenly, as if in wait,
faint hints of browning are upon them.

Some baptisms are much more shocking—
a sudden dip in a muddy watering hole,

much before there is understanding,
before a newly born can exercise

a choice. For me, in Oklahoma, I was
almost twelve, full of disbeliefs—

I never believed in the great depression,
in the great war, or that the best of the

top soil would ever return. I simply
believed in a better life somewhere else.

But somehow I lost the war, and the pond
event was much too sudden, much too

muddy, offering nothing to clear my mind.

With Resignation

the old maple tree begins to write
its fall treatise: each falling leaf

claiming a figure of speech, a
sentence, a paragraph, a subject

heading, a kernel of thought,
each one demanding its due

of recognition, emphasis. This
is how the old maple broadcasts

and broadcasts against the hum
of the winds. Today it will take

more than howlings to deny
what it has patiently learned over

the seasons: all the lessons of
waiting, all the benefits of giving.

Soon After The Break

in the heavy cloud cover, the eyes
are drawn toward the bright West,

to occasional tarns of sunlight
claiming vacancies in the trees,

vacancies that shift with each
new angle of light; they are the

transitory jewels of afternoon,
given to us on the downslope of day,

stark reminders of the other side
that is always there, waiting.

The Irises

In November, in the middle of this
indecision of weather, I find them,

iridescent, cloistered in a cluster
of long grass around the privet tree,

where they always return with their
blooming whenever curiosity gets

the better. It is magnificent how
they find those deep and cerulean

blues and arrange them so wholly
around and through the whites,

how they put on those enchanting
dapplings, those touches of yellow

with which they lay claim to charms
and charming. Such contrast in these

grasses gives new meaning to bunching,
to any procreative start, caught

in the light, brought to fruition.
This kneeling, this close inspection,

this admiration, is a kind of prayer,
an acceptance of blessing, of something

bestowed, inviolable.

The Day After

the record cold, I found the iris
in the cluster around the camphor tree

half asleep, a near canopy of cobalt
blueness over the rasp of winter's sorrow.

It was then I felt the need to walk away
from the magnetic pull of it, to grapple

with something deep, a longing
I suddenly felt for summer.

Icicles In The Pyracantha

hang on the berries, with more ice
clumping them into clusters that are

intimate, into twisted marriages. Yet
they are filled with sparkle in the bright

sun, as if eager to attract and hold
the eyes of the curious, eager to sport,

to assert their overnight dress of ice
that is their full projection. They revel

in their shimmer, continue to steal
a bit of glory that will not last.

Terzanelle For The Advent Of Winter

There is no need to count leaves now;
the leaves of the apricot have flown.
The brutal winds have shown us how.

No longer are the days so long.
Our nights predominate the mind.
The leaves of the apricot have flown.

The rising mists are now so kind
they shroud the nakedness of trees.
But nights predominate the mind.

New burdens fall upon the leaves;
the dank and dreary curses grow.
Mists shroud the nakedness of trees.

Our lights of night emit their glow.
We learn to huddle, do our best,
as dank and dreary curses grow.

We must work through this winter's test.
We learn to huddle, do our best.
There is no need to count leaves now;
the brutal winds have shown us how.

Notes On The Evening Of A Poem

The evening is closing in the West,
darkening clouds beginning to shut down

the sun. The gaps between dark cloud
and dark cloud closing, closing.

So much so that, after a while,
only a slither of sun remains.

In the West of the departing sun
my heart hungers, almost refusing

to let it go.

Poem Of The Night Of Observation Of A Particular Moon

Simply a sliver of moon, a mere sliver,
curling towards its quarters, in its universe

of partially-seens, giving little away
of distance, and almost nothing of the

total numbers of which it is merely one,
one of a quadrillion of lit and unlit ghosts

shadowing one or the other of them.
So what, then, should I make of this startling

particular, this guidepost to my nights,
my seasons, this hope that things really

have a definitive place, a time that will
remain for a while, as I can only be

at comfort in the shadows of it, little,
almost infinitesimal me.

More Against Forgetting In Somewhat Less Than A Season

I'll not forget, never forget the confused
covers of night, the elliptical coverings

of night, the bright full moon we now
know was occluded, out of position,

not above the houses that were or weren't
upon the whims of man and woman, too,

their domains eminent and imminent,
even as the huge machines were moving

and digging, excavating and blowing
the very earth, trembling earth around us.

Yes, remember how the night covers
left dismissively, disdainfully, exposing

a nakedness, hardly a curiosity now,
as the night itself loosened its hold.

Ellipsis of night, entanglement, entwinement,
of covers tossed into hysterical piles, or

rolled carelessly aside past separated knees,
past anxious thighs, against all the conjurings

of imagination, dreamings of the demands
of night: penetrating, interpenetrating,

almost nothing left against the will of
intrusion, almost nothing left of comfort,

only those things that abandoned fears
lead to in their final acts of closure.

Laverne Frith is a regular member of the Reviewer Panel of the New York Journal of Books. His reviews of poets such as Mary Oliver, Frank Bidart, and Jorie Graham appear regularly on the *NYJB* Website. Links to his reviews have also appeared on the National Book Critics Circle blog, *Critical Mass.*

Laverne is co-editor and founder of *Ekphrasis: A Poetry Journal,* the premier publication comprised exclusively of poems about works of art. In addition, Laverne was, for nineteen years, the monthly poetry columnist for the widely circulated *Living in the West/Senior Magazine.*

Laverne has a number of other published chapbooks, including three from Finishing Line Press (two nominated for the California Book Awards), and a unique chapbook, *Celebrations: Images and Texts* (Rattlesnake Press, 2009), which features Frith's photography as well as his poetry. He was Runner-up for the 2004, 2005, & 2006 *Louisiana Literature* Prize in Poetry. His first full-length collection, *Imagining the Self,* was published by Cherry Grove Collections in 2011. His second full-length collection, *The Evaporating Hours,* was released from AuthorsPress, India (2015). His poetry has appeared in *The Christian Science Monitor, Sundog* (The Southeast Review), *The Sow's Ear Poetry Review, Memoir Journal, California Quarterly, The Dalhousie Review, Common Ground Review, Blue Unicorn, Maryland Poetry Review, Permafrost: A Literary Journal,* and numerous other publications in the U.S. and abroad. Laverne's poetry has been choreographed and performed at the California Palace of the Legion of Honor in San Francisco. He has presented many workshops on poetry subjects over the years.

CPSIA information can be obtained at www.ICGtesting.com
Printed in the USA
BVOW05s0140200516

448700BV00001B/6/P